Choose Lethe:
Remember to Forget

poems by

Carolyn Clark

Finishing Line Press
Georgetown, Kentucky

Choose Lethe:
Remember to Forget

Copyright © 2018 by Carolyn Clark
ISBN 978-1-63534-469-1 First Edition
All rights reserved under International and Pan-American Copyright Conventions. No part of this book may be reproduced in any manner whatsoever without written permission from the publisher, except in the case of brief quotations embodied in critical articles and reviews.

ACKNOWLEDGMENTS

I would like to thank the following presses for their publication of these individual poems in previous versions:

Avocet (*The Avocet Weekly*): "Nones: Morning Song," "Twig Poem"
Cayuga Lake Books: "Clean," "Porch Wood," "Hope is in the Healing," "De Amicitia," "One Day You Wake Up," Exhalations on a Power Line, "Moon Blind Mare," "Remember to Forget"

Published in my book of collected poems, *New Found Land* (Cayuga Lake Books, 2017): "Clean"; "De Amicitia"; "Exhalations on a Power Line"; "Hope is in the Healing"; "Moon Blind Mare"; "Nones: Morning Song"; "One Day You Wake Up: Upstate"; "Porch Wood"; "Remember to Forget"; "Twig Poem"

A special thank you to friends and family as readers, and especially to my mother Florence Clark (poet), and father Mills Gardner Clark, may he rest in peace.

Publisher: Leah Maines
Editor: Christen Kincaid
Cover Photo: Geoffrey Cullen
Author Photo: Geoffrey Cullen
Cover Design: Elizabeth Maines McCleavy

Printed in the USA on acid-free paper.
Order online: www.finishinglinepress.com
also available on amazon.com

Author inquiries and mail orders:
Finishing Line Press
P. O. Box 1626
Georgetown, Kentucky 40324
U. S. A.

Table of Contents

Clean 1

An Introduction: I am a Writer 2

After Bath 3

Catalyst Daughter 4

Porch Wood 5

Hope is in the Healing 6

Twig Poem 7

Shadowboxing 8

Beta 9

Winter 10

Word Scythe 11

Augusts Cross Section 12

De Amicitia 13

Nones: Morning Song 14

One Day You Wake Up 15

Black Friday by the Barn 16

Exhalations on a Power Line 17

Moon Blind Mare 20

The Barn on Snyder Hill 22

Remember to forget 26

to all the children

Clean

I wash myself under
waterfall of sound:

thrush, wind, wood,
dreams swim away.

Clock resonance matches
the tick of thicket birds

while my new day's gait
brushes grass.

An Introduction: I am a Writer
(Connecticut Avenue, D.C., 1986)

I am a writer. I was ten when I first learned this.
At more than twice that age I'd denied it for a dozen years
and at least that many reasons. Perhaps I was overwhelmed
by the bright lights of patriarchs
who ranged like a winking tapestry of saints
far beyond the dark ages and into the Classics.
Even though I'd read works by women writers,
from Madeleine L'Engle to Sappho,
I could not be stirred from my silent reception:
reading such genius bade me bite my tongue.
But this reverence for things near and old
was not alone to silence me.
A strange mix of pride and humiliation
caused me to become a self-appointed Philomela:
a stupid pride (false humiliation?)
to have touched the fringe of this ancient shawl
in its native weave of Latin or Greek
sustained my notion that my own work amounted to nothing.
And indeed, through the sad, long eyelashes of history,
mine will be invisible: a child's garden of verses, born and abandoned.

Yet strange things have been known to occur…a child's coloring book,
the play of light and dark against a wall, may spring out
in hardy bloom,
ignoring colorless boundaries
to climb sea cliffs
in heliotropic health.
But for too long
I lived in the lower seas
as a pale yellow
foraging sponge
upon the ocean floor.
I didn't know that yellow was also a color
for a rose,
         and noon
                  and lions.

After Bath

Her breath crowding the mirror,
she leans into the fog.

Under water her fingers
close in on the cold,

in the air her fist
unfolds:

*in one flick
a thousand faces born—*

little beads
contain her smile,

she watches as they slide
through the steam.

Catalyst daughter

Yes I know
I am the catalyst
for catastrophe.
The whole house is
mumbling with flowers.
On the piano
covered with grandmother's
paisley shawl full of motion,
Emotion is framed by nettles
picked last winter:
Queen Anne's Lace placed
by a slender hand
that plucks pagan clover
from the back garden.
Rain or shine, Mom walks
and finds time for things
that I desire.
Supper always at six
—mother father sister brother—
a blessing recited in straight lines,
hands folded, heads bowed to pasta—
a substance of a life
lost, once found, in Italy:
leftovers from overseas.
The silence that never was.
Her chatter is like a monkey
that never climbs down.
Her face still shines
of the moon over Naples'
celebrated Blue Grotto, light
angling through schools
of tiny silver fish, backs and bronzed shoulders
slipping a rowboat under the cave.
Aquatic opulence.
Peace? If only we could.
Envious? Let's speed things up!
I am the catalyst daughter,
find my rate of reaction!

Porch Wood

On our long lost way
to cut the Christmas tree
the back roads splintered into shortcuts
only a mule could know.

Way back
from macadam roads the wooden shack
looked silvery in frozen sunlight,
yet its quartered wood stacked high
upon a seaboard porch
spoke preparation.

Winters never were like this,
everyone said, in Georgia,
but the board house knew,
it knew better,
whoever dared live there,
knew each chimney brick.

How long this house had howled,
nobody knew.
But a pig and a dog
on the lee side of the ditch
shared tangled cover in the naked berries
until the cold snap passed,
and porch wood
once again
sparked the hearth.

Hope is in the healing

Hope is in the healing,
the looking up
when the horse trips
going over the triple spread.

Remember what the Good Book says:

keep your chin up
and be grateful
for the forgiving ground,

the dark tumble of earth
that absorbs
the curl of our spines
as we roll
earthbound
in an indoor ring

where the ground
is not frozen
this winter,

and like memory,
keeps coming back
to me.

Twig Poem
    for Archie Ammons (Chamonix, 1978)

Motions spring
from melting snow: a twig regains consciousness,
weight released from former state.
Support comes from the main stem
as things begin to loosen.
Corn snow we call it back home,
hard buds whose melting makes way for motion.

Each day another layer of destruction is
revealed: littered needles, lichen,
moss on thirsty rock. But today it's a long, poised twig
that traps my eye.

Older stuff would have cracked,
but not this green! It knows to breathe in
the deep mountain crystalline
and make no bones about it.
It's high time to start growing again
to higher stature, saturated
in an optical osmosis
some call breath, others air.
And so I say, where is there not change?
A twig breaks out
without even breaking,
with just enough force
to kick aside snow,
keeping me still, astonished.

There's a story behind every bump in nature:
sudden jumps have their reason.

The morning sun did nothing unusual,
just continued to bleed
its winter cloak away
till new life sprung seed
from water: a *twig* that throws *corn snow!*

Shadowboxing Diana
(Sciamachia—slashing at shades of the dead)

Tenuous uppermost reaches of trees,
the movement of your upturned hands
still clings like perfume to my temples.

Tremulous me,
running out self-made hoops
while half-hoping
a poem in your image
might impress on two-faced stone
some permanence.

Once we ignore
autumn's clamoring song
clarion death etches in
right from wrong.

Ask the tamarack
why she pines,
and the gold leaf
stripped from its vine.

Ask why I still run
elliptical miles
like a soldier whom war has deserted,
has no song,
cannot be at ease,
still running from shadows,
stumbling over oak roots
in the forest.

Beta:

Brush away erasure's flesh,
clear the table, rejoice:
Real god came to grant us choice
from soul's recessive sorrow, breath!

No more cliché latchkey children
and forgotten gloom.
Bring in light to all fruition:
evil is but absence and abysmal fear.

Into a well-lit room we march,
mercifully entrenched in tunnel vision,
like a knotted serpent offering fruit
in Aesclepion proscription,
mindful of our sprawling roots,
the thirsting of a baobab tree
and our little prince.

What's a Classic?
Circuitous demands
traveling both directions
in chameleon-like blindness,

as the fig worm wrestles
in its sea of similarity
blending into that womb
where expectations meet reality:

*just because you cannot see it
doesn't mean it isn't there.*

---

* Alpha is in *Mnemosyne: The Long Traverse* (2013)

Winter

This morning for breakfast:
a corn muffin sun
steaming inside,
outside,
a long skirt of winter.

Word Scythe: Wind River
    for Nina

What is this dusty voice
kicked up from fallen leaves?

Fresh September
intrudes on our senses,
sharpens the word scythe
that ever follows fullness.

Corn not yet reaped
stands in dusky rows
rattling dry husks
while in the kitchen
famine-defying *Penates*,
crickets of all sizes,
sentinel the sink.

Images edge out
and fray,
old cut-offs
fringed in summer's bleach,
still hot.

Autumnal sun
spicy as paprika
summons her aging children,
seeds that slough off
steep mud banks where
shimmery cottonwoods
yield their shade
to spindly spores,

whose whitened dancers
foil to follow
the river wind round.

Augusts Cross Section
for Audrey—and Pindie

Augusts cross section neatly,
like growth on a lumbered tree:
the memory stump betrays summers' increase.

This is a lean summer for the South.
Its drought shall be remembered in more
than these annals of fingernail width.

Yet to me in the watery tropics
of our nation's capital,
drought is an absence beyond imagining.

It is as unimaginable
as an empty church on Sunday,
as fuzzy as an unclean lens.

This morning, guilt-tinged but irrefutable,
a tear sprung from my left eye
as the moon shaped sacrament

melted on my palate,
for I knew its color
was that of wet sand:

my thoughts were with
the shimmer of northern beaches,
Menemsha, Gay Head, and images of freedom.

De Amicitia
    for Audrey

Picking
snarly snaps
in a drought,
hair bleached out,
you're still honoring
your commitments:
a wedding tomorrow,
footprints in sand,
a honeymoon that memory never erased,
and an extra pair that appeared like an angel,
kept going.

Like this one more row
of snapdragons,
seemingly endless,
dusty yet so alive,
thirsty and not knowing
where the line break is,
or just where
one row begins
and another ends,

because with you, A.
it's just not that way,
and maybe that is why

you keep them
growing.

Nones: **Morning song**
(Nones: Roman 5th or 7th of the month)

Somewhere
in the morning swirl,
leaving home,
a sluggish squirrel
near wheels and whirl—

scrunched away!
and Saturday with all its hopes
unfurled:
none other than this
morning song,
morning song!

Somewhere
beneath
a veil lifted
from gray business
and saved me
from the humdrum,
the neck aches,
the ashes of yesterdays'
hearth fire.

A song unexpected,
a brief reminder that no more
"your time will come"
or "time will tell"
could cure me
of this morning song,
this self,
moving
from the yawning hiatus,

whether it be *Nones*
or unknowns.

One day you wake up
> *(1977, upon hearing how Prof. McConkey and his wife chose a place to settle down)*

One day you wake up
to what this place is really about.

You check out the scene,
then, having scouted around,
you realize you'll have to leave…

unless you marry into the small town myth
of agrarian endings,

unless that ox-head falls off your engine hood

and you realize
the anchor's in the soil
for good,
and you start out

      with four good eyes.

Black Friday by the Barn
a paean for Sarah and Josh, 2013

The best things in life are not for sale.
Stayin' off the Pike,
the bridle trails are closed
"due to wet conditions."
I need sunshine on my face,
park the yellow Bug near a mud paddock,
facing southwest.
The winter sun is right about
where Venus has been appearing
these evenings of late, wearing her halo,
unearthly bright.
I'm still tracking her…but today is Black Friday.
I sit and sift through what's not on sale:
yesterday's race memories,
and a new old pain in my big toe.
Tonight, at a leftovers party,
my old best friend, N. our hostess,
will lavish well-deserved praise
on all our daughters and sons.
How they succeed!
Even when they fail, they heal.
For now I'll just sit still,
warm in the winter sun,
in the yellow Beetle, a chrysalis
bundled in yesterday's memories
before they too fly away.
For in this umpteenth
Turkey Chase since 1982
who can say when if ever
true loves both have come in first—
in Age Group and Overall?
I'll bet just once.
Once upon a time…
that's how a story begins: *olim* (once)—
since times Roman, some things happen
but once: *the things no money can buy.*

Exhalations on a Power Line

I.

My first day off school I drop my daughter at Jet Blue,
saddle up the horse, head towards the Giant by way of the woods.
Bright dew shines in long grass up the power line,
a solo purple morning glory thrusts out from blackberries' edge,
concave silvery nets scattered like mini trampolines
wedge between damp weeds and stray buckling wheat.
Today I turn away to take it all in, go past to explore
the spotless grounds of the nearby Primitive Baptist Church:
daintily we skirt their fresh Meeting House,
slow between two wells, slip past the green graveyard,
until I glimpse a small headstone whose words are barely worn:
a couple died two years apart (1876—1924/1926)
not so uncommon: his story became hers, lost and found.

II.

I think of my granddad outliving two wives,
parachuting with the Red Cross at fifty-five
how he alone swam the Sauer
under machinegun fire,
twice out, twice back,
in long johns, on his waist a rope
to tie around the far shore's tree,
line for a bridge,
saving untold lives.
No official soldier,
but on the down low
President Truman slipped him
a Bronze Star.

III.

Emboldened, we head back
to the power line
for a little lope,
then a fiery hand-gallop
up soft, dark, earthen trails,
slowing to dainty across pot shards
and broken glass
leached out from old soil
by fresh-cut ruts,
jarred open
from the recent plague—
dirt bikes.
Our simple horse trail
has been taken over,
multiplied into looped knots.
The screaming ATV's
create faux creek beds,
crack dried mud pools,
scatter rock, strip roots from earth
made smooth and slippery
as a wet gym floor.
Toward the top of our loop,
slowing from canter to trot—
there's an unmistakable sound: "Bees!"
big-bodied wasps streamline, keep our pace,
three or four, …don't count, don't look back!
Move out! into extended trot,
knock through even these roots
so fast we can lose them.
And we do come through
as from a dream,
whistling soft as prayer.

The morning's quiet now holds the usual sounds:
cars whir, trucks grind. But our mare, Sister Leto,
in her familiar language
snorts three times, walks loosely, well knows
that now
we're headed home.

Moon blind mare

Diagnosis is a Greek word
(as is anything that ends in "-*is*").

My best friend for twelve years
turned twice that age
but within the span of two raggedy autumns
she—Leopard Appaloosa that she *is*—
developed recurring *uvitis*.
Her eye was twice daily anointed
with triple antibiotics
named from ancient (Greek) roots:
Op*ti*mune, Flurbi*profen*, Atro*pine*.
She grazes unflinchingly,
keeps her head down, all business.
Hungry as a bear, that mare!
Had she been one of Diomedes'
flesh-eating fillies we'd all be dead!
Admittedly, Sister Leto *is* a bit indifferent
to my call in all seasons—except winter.
And she comes into season
every moon, stands by the geldings' pasture gate,
nickers and flirts.
Her BFF is a Blanket App about half her age.
In winter her white coat brightens,
blends with snow when she runs into the wind,
and she used to move faster than spit can freeze.

Progno*sis* for Moon Blindn*ess*?
Many remedies but no cure… the mystery is
there *is* no cure *for this* oldest documented disease
among domesticated animals:
ancient Egyptians first recorded their dismay
at the sudden loss of sight in healthy horses,

inexplicable and random
as plague-bearing arrows
borne by far-shooting Apollo.
We now only know that Moon Blindness
occurs most often in Paints and Apps.

The Irish still believe a white horse *is* magical.
So our S*i*ster, she is just that,
though it's all we can do
to keep her right eye alive.
For the left eye is
too late to bring back:
faded blue globe, icy pale,
the color of old denim,
but still blinking..

At night under twinkling stars
I come out to the barn late
to see how she's doing.
I find her easily,
immortal, green but gentle,
warm my hands in her barrel chest,
cross under her neck and sing
"My Bonnie lies over the ocean…"
tired and teary, but happy just to be there,
knowing that she still knows
just who and where *I am.*

The Barn on Snyder Hill *

The girl pulled the car up alongside the gray barn doors, turned off the motor and sat looking for a moment straight ahead at the rusty rings that girdled the base of the silo. The snow had drifted up against the window which in summer let in cobwebbed light into the manger. The girl placed a scarf on her hair and then lowered her head to tie the knot in back, catching the hairs and not caring, and then opening the car door and breathing openmouthed the cold air until her teeth hurt, and the new car smell was instantly squelched. She walked through the drifts toward the fence, noticing how the snow clung to her jeans and knowing it would soon melt into her boots.

She slipped through the wood fence and walked with attempted smoothness toward the barn, calling softly to the horses so they would not bang their heads as they backed out of the stanchions, wild eyed with surprise.

From this side of the silo she could see into the barn and by the vague movements towards the back she knew the horses were in, away from the sunlight. She bent at the waist and one leg after another slipped through the fence and called to the horses as she walked toward the darkness. She did not like to surprise them into a panic, banging their cheekbones against the stanchion boards and rolling their eyes as they tried to back out of the hay. The shyest horse, the wild-eyed mare, Gypsy, was the first to come running out towards the girl and then away into the snow, to stand and snort for a while, or sometimes to watch quietly with large suspicious eyes. The mare's large daughter, Alika, always had to be pushed back from the hay.

Inside the barn was warm and sweet, the winter's manure spread high and firm over the old barn floor. The horses were watching, so she pushed the largest one back from the hay and slipped sideways through the stanchions. In the tack room white light from outside filtered through the old boards of the tack room wall. She took a blue-and-white halter and lead off the top of a tin can on the wall and retraced her steps towards the chestnut mare, Emily. In the corner where the manure was high she was careful of the horse's head close to the whitewashed beam in the ceiling.

She circled the neck with right arm and, halter in hand, pushed the soft nose into its circle and fastened the halter on the left, pressing her face against the warm fur. Then she was outside again in the blinding sunlight, leading her horse to the gate, pulling the aluminum slide bar back and untangling the bailing twine with fingers quickly growing cold, opening the gate wide enough so as not to bang the mare's hipbone, then closing the gate quickly to keep the other horses from following. Her back turned from the horse, sliding the bar back into place with a clang, she felt the impatient tugging from behind, as the horse tugged expectantly toward the familiar post where she was fed. The girl felt the power of the horse in her hands.

With a quick-release knot the girl tied her up to the fence post across from the rusted pump piled with snow and left her pawing. She walked toward the grain room, feeling her back being watched, unhooked the latch, and with her fingers around the back of the door swung it out slowly against a tapered snowdrift, watching the smooth flat arc appear like the wing of a snow angel. She stepped over it and into the tack room where the snow had drifted in a little from the sides and fallen down the ladder from the silo. The saddles were covered with empty burlap grain bags, and winter clothes were in bundles on the shelf.

Looking out the barn's small window she could see her horse pawing. How pretty she looked, with her neck arched and her foot pawing and coat rich chestnut against the snow! The girl scooped a couple of quarts of oats into the bucket and another quart of corn. She took a small grooming kit trunk off the shelf, picked up the bucket, and, taking each by the handle, walked back out into the snow. She set the trunk down and with a piece of bailing twine tied the bucket handle to the fence (the horse had a habit of spilling her oats) and began picking her feet. The wind had cleaned the pond that day, and its ice came out in one big chunk, shaped to the sole of her feet.

Underneath the sole was wet and tight, especially the one white foot, healthy but slightly shriveled and the girl laughed aloud as she thought of her horse in a dishwashing ad. When the horse was finished and she held the bucket so the horse could get the very last before taking it back inside and setting the little grooming trunk back on the shelf. She reached for the bridle and martingale and they slid easily onto her shoulder. She took the grain bag off the English saddle. She picked it up and then balanced it on her left arm, lightly holding the cantle with her right hand, and hurried smoothly back to the horse where she laid the saddle on the withers and slid it back into place. She unhooked the halter, slid it off her nose and hooked it again around her neck.

Then, watching the cold air curl dragon-like from the horse's nostrils, she remembered the cold and her hand went to the bit. How cold it would be against the horse's warm tongue! The girl held the bit of the bridle in her hands, rubbing it and then holding it, then tried again rubbing it warm and then holding it close to her own lips to breathe warmth into the cold steel. When the bit no longer numbed her bare skin she looped the reins and the martingale over the horse's head, and then, holding the bit in her left hand and the crown of the bridle in her right, she held the bridle up and fed the horse the bit. She pulled each ear through one by one and then the forelock. She fastened the throatlatch and then went to the saddle, throwing the girth over, moving under the neck of the horse and checking the other side, unfolding the saddle pad and untwisting the girth.

She dove back under the horse's neck again and on the left again reached under the belly, pushing the girth through the loop on the martingale and then standing with the girth buckles at chest level and with her right elbow holding up the saddle flap, the girl pulled as tight as she could, waited and then pulled again, kneeing the horse in the belly as she tightened the girth and buckled it.

Then she pulled down on the stirrup and the horse knew when she was free from around the neck and began to walk forward, impatient. The girl, also impatient, pulled her back as she slid the stirrup down. From the drift above the horse she mounted: she held the horse still in the snow next to the road and mounted quickly. Even as her leg swung around the flank she felt the horse move forward but did not stop her, feeling awkward and happy sliding the other stirrup down as they started down the road.

*for Mrs. Whicher's English class (1974): describe something you know well

Remember to forget: choosing *Lethe*

Remember to forget:
lithe bodies,
nimble minds,
the sticky notes
that bind us
beyond our control,
Dad's ubiquitous
Don't Forget notes
all over the house,
our sole phone's
black curly cord
shining with voices
untangled if pulled
under the hall
bathroom door
where on the throne
we daughters adapted
conversational tones
to the faucet murmur,
beyond his earshot,
yet still umbilical.

Entrenched behind
his rough cut pine board,
he invented the first laptop.
Brow raised, head down,
his *Oh-my-aching-back*
supported by curvature
of a uniquely dehisced
rust-orange Citroen chair,
Dad often read for hours,
underlined in red,
then would date, clip, tape and place
the consumed victims
into wire baskets

until, troughs spilling over,
clippings systemically disappeared
into bulging green vertical files
near his big desk
in our living room.
Dad faced the sidewalk,
curtains open, sentinel.
Oversize art books
layered in a niche to his left,
Encyclopedia Britannica
tightly vertical on his right,
soldiers at attention.
next to the vestibule,
the front hall closet.
Now Dad sits
with his back
to the window
in a wing chair
in someone else's house,
holds a sky blue
plastic velvet lap desk
where he reads big print books,
turning page after page,
marks time with a well-placed
laminated bookmark,
its pressed flowers chosen
by a watchful woman,
his wife of sixty some years.

You ask what can he remember?

Last autumn when I asked him
what are you thinking of?
Dad looked with a smile,
uttered two words
Buddha-style:

Perfect Love.

Carolyn Clark (Ph.D. Classics), was born in Ithaca, NY and periodically lived in Italy, Switzerland and France. She studied poetry under Archie Ammons and earned a B.A. in Classical Civilization from Cornell, a Masters degree in Classics at Brown and eventually completed a doctorate at Johns Hopkins, *Tibullus Illustrated: Lares, Genius and Sacred Landscapes* (C.C. Breen, Baltimore, UMI 1998). After three decades of teaching Latin and French in Maryland, she now focuses primarily on poetry (*Amish Mimesis*, 2015; *New Found Land*, 2017).

This chapbook inverses the themes of her first Finishing Line Press poetry publication *Mnemosyne: The Long Traverse* (2013). The cover photo is a view of their pasture after a summer storm.

www.ingramcontent.com/pod-product-compliance
Lightning Source LLC
LaVergne TN
LVHW041511070426
835507LV00012B/1485